Praise
Liz Dolan

Liz Dolan writes about the past with and eye and ear tuned to the poetry of the ordinary, unencumbered by the sentimentality of nostalgia, but filled with the emotion made from the real ties between people and their communities, their landscapes, their times. There's loveliness here, the gritty kind, the sparse kind and the joyous kind too.

—Gerry LaFemina
Author of *Little Heretic* and *Notes for the Novice Ventriloquist*

Each poem in *A Secret of Long Life* stands up for itself like a sturdy Catholic school girl: no pretense, no posturing. Not to say the poems are simple—not at all. These poems are the work of a skilled and deeply thoughtful poet. Dolan knows how to let a family's history—of Ireland and the Bronx and the Delaware beaches—tell its profound and nuanced truths.

—Fleda Brown
Former Poet Laureate of Delaware and author of *No Need of Sympathy*

Haunted and haunting, these poems thrum and trill with memory, keen with sorrow, and are always brimming with life. Liz Dolan has written a beautiful collection!

—Julianna Baggott
Author of *Pure*

洞月亮

CAVE MOON PRESS
YAKIMA 中 WASHINGTON

2014

A Secret of Long Life

A Secret of Long Life

Liz Dolan

洞月亮

CAVE MOON PRESS

YAKIMA 中 WASHINGTON

Acknowledgements

Ancient Paths, Barrel House, Bard Song, Blast Furnace, Canadian Woman's Studies, Dappled Things, Delaware Beach Life, Delaware Poetry Review, Delmarva Review, Dreamstreets, Ducts, Illuminations, Labletter, Literary Mama, Literary House Review, Mudlark, Natural Bridge, New Delta Review, Philadelphia Stories, Prism International Quarterly UBC, Red River Review, Referential, SLAB, Spindle, The Broadkill Review, The Cortland Review, The Littoral Zone, The Mom Egg, The Nassau Review, The Naugatuck Review, The Other Journal, The Pedestal, Your Daily Poem, Cobalt Review

Anthologies:

Advice My Mother Gave Me, Love Notes, Miracles and Extraordinary Blessings, Mourning Anthology, The Kennedy Curse, The Newborn Anthology, Poetry in the Cathedral, Token Entry, Unruly Catholic Women Writers

Liz would like to acknowledge her colleagues at The Rehoboth Art League's Writers' Group for their poetic insights.

A very special thank you to my mentors Julianna Baggott, Fleda Brown, and especially Gerry Lafemina.

The photograph on the cover depicts my mother's Aunt Nellie on The Stoney Lonen in Tullaree, Kilcoo, County Down where my mother's beautiful soul was nurtured and tempered with steel. It was taken in 1965.

Dedication

For my husband, for all my children and my brother and sisters

Table of Contents

Acknowledgements   ix
Dedication   x

Part One

Sepia Photo   1
Lost Child   2
A Mother to Her Daughter   4
Deliver Us   5
Ordinary Things   7
Air Raid Drills   8
The Boy Who Swings on Our Line   9
On Winter Evenings Father Strings the Moon   11
The House That Ruth Built   12
Picking Up Steam   14
The Day My Father's Father Died   15
I Longed to Be as Lovely   16
Mary Has Chosen   17
Great Expectations   18
For My Best Friend 1950   19
Casting Aspersions   20
My Friends Had Nothing   21
Death Reels   22
How I Loved the Way Sister Hooked Up   23

Part Two

The Florist Gave Me Gifts   27
The Life You Save   28
Saturday at F. W. Woolworth's   29
Sunday at the German Bakery   30
Holy Day   32

For Once I Am Able to Save Her   34
A Hot Time   35
Tonight I Let My Brother In   37

Part Three

Fat in the Can   41
Rose Hawthorne Creates   42
Teresa of Avila, Mystic, Reformer, Exhorts Her Sisters   43
Stunned By Charismatics at Evening Mass   44
A Wife To Her Dying Husband   45
My Old Man Couldn't Even Die Quiet   46
Offering   47
Caught Unaware   48
Driving to School   49
The Man Who Loved His Mother-in-Law   50
An August Place   51
My Second Pair of Eyes   52
What I Did Not Say   53
Interruptions   53
Virtue Rewarded   56
What Is Hardest   57
Lessons   59

Part Four

Early Sorrow   63
The Healing   64
Child Inside the Mirror   65
Dos Diablos   66
My Three Year Old Grandson Has Down   67
Grace   69
The Fall   70

Sleep Over Parties   71
In My Dream   72
The Lady of Annie B Street Is Gone   73
How to Deconstruct a Home   74
The White–Washed Cottage   76
The Spelling Test   77
The House on Overing Street   78
Words Sprout Wings   79
A Secret of Long Life   80

About the Author   82
About the Charity   83

Part One

Sepia Photo-One Room Schoolhouse, 1917

In the highest row stands Master Breen
his hands folded like Cuchulain across his chest.
His mustache tips brush up against his checked cravat,
My mother-auburn haired and girlish- stands to his left
in brogues and a coarse wool dress she sewed herself.
At ten each morn she serves her master tea.

I beg her, Stay in Tullaree forever.
You'll miss the warmth of the cows' udders
and the bleating sheep in the upper pasture.
Don't cross the sea, Mama.
You'll scrub until your knuckles bleed
pink tears on our white blouses;
you'll dust and sweep with Yeats
turned to stone in your chest.
Your son's head will be crushed,
three infants will die. Your husband, another master
you will serve, will wax as thorny as pyracantha.
                          *
Cushla, at Eastertide sixteen patriots were shot
in Dublin. I'm a papist scullion in Ulster
which soon will be chopped off like a gangrened arm.
My brother will inherit the land. You've never been starved
by the wind from the banks of the Bann. You choose
your masters in this life. Our whispered faith,
sustained as we knelt on nettles, will gird me
like the radiant skin of a snake.

Lost Child

On a hot June afternoon,
fives and nines on the board,

loose-limbed and floating-free,
Sister's voice thrumming,

I place my head upon my desk,
press my ear to the cool wood,

hear the thump, thump, thump
of the little men,

Come, come, come, wee flaxy girl.
I slip my purpled fingers

into the hollow inkwell hole
where, in coats of white and silver

and hats of red foxglove,
they whisk me into the hushed, dark wood,

the souls of my own dead
thick as bees about me.

Inch high fairies, translucent as silk,
spun on dewdrops, sup

fresh bread, fresh butter, sweet peaches in cream.
A three-thumbed fiddler

springs a reel while hand in hand,
ringing the hawthorn tree, they lilt

Far, Far Be Hell's Black Viper,
and *The Wind that Shakes the Barley,*

uillean pipes on the breeze,
apple blossoms in my hair.

A Mother to Her Daughter

Dig the peat from beneath
his ragged nails and file them smooth.
Air the upper room, the crocheted spread.

' Tis a pity to bury him
in his store-boughten suit
when the Devlins down the lonen
go threadbare through the bog of a Sunday.

      I can no thole your tears, child.
                  ' Twere no saint he.
His long silences hogged my light.
Dust on chintz curtains. Draw well
water for tea. Fetch a porcelain cup.
   Arra, Cushla, hush,
                save a sup for him.
' Tweren't it he that was always starved
                    with the cold.

Deliver Us

When mother was wee
the midwife Big Mary
trudged down the lonen
bundled in a black cape
billowed by winds off the Irish Sea
whistling through black night
over the roof of the flax mill
shaking the red barn's shingles.

On their table, flat bread, fresh butter
and red berries in clotted cream glowed
while over kindling crackling
in the Kilcoo hearth, water roiled blue.

Her cheeks persimmon, barely able to
kneel still, mother
prayed with her father
befuddled when he squeezed her
fingers til blackthorn beads
chafed. From her mother's groans
in the lower room she kenned
she would soon snuggle
the nursling Big Mary had carried

under her cape. Years later,
across the waters
far from the mountain rill
spilling past mother's cottage,
cape-less doctors and starched nurses
with radiant tools
delivered three of her bairn
dead, shrouded by a white room
in a cast iron, barred-bed.
A silver-embossed radiator hissed
beneath a brick-walled window.

Ordinary Things   New York, 1942

He smoothes the brim of his grey fedora
and hands Mr. Mulligan a crisp twenty,
a ten and a five for the white pine box.
I will carry it myself, he says.
And he does, to the bedroom where
the boy dressed in his cotton suit
lies on mother's crocheted spread.
He places the body in the satin-lining
as if he were laying out Sunday clothes,
sets a tiny prayer book in his broken fingers.
He tucks a cat's eye marble and a red hot
in his vest pocket and stares at him,
then opens the window so he can
taste the bitter air and hear
the flutter of dotted-Swiss curtains.

Air Raid Drills

As a child, I was drawn to air raid drills
which wimpled, rat-faced Sister Reparata
orchestrated from her desk,
a break in the routine
of folded hands and numbing notes.
We scrambled under our desks
heads tucked, knees bent
like blue and white turtles
retreating into our shells.

Who would drop a bomb on us?

My terrified classmate, Joyce Ostraticky,
wept into her navy blue taffeta tie.
She longed for the Holy Father to open
the letter—Russia converted—
through prayers to Mary.
She smiled down on us,
the yellow daisies we brought
strewn at her foot
crushing the head of the serpent.

The Boy Who Swings on Our Line

My cauled eyes open to the fluttering
sheets fanned by my brother's

ansty five-year-old soul. From the open window
I see as he swells my father's overalls,

crooks the knees and bellows as though
with Dad he flags the six a.m. from Darien.

He puffs up breasts in my Peter-panned
school blouse. Luciferous boy. He snuggles

in my mother's tea-rosed house coat,
twists his v-necked Yankee shirt

about the line, now worn by his relief,
a baby brother. Beware of trucks, I whisper,

much too late. Does anyone else know he's here?
He grasps my mother's sage-scented hands

as she snaps each piece of bleached laundry
and pins it to his trapeze. I am not sure

if I want him to stay and play. I lie.
Go, release us all from your awful presence,

airborne shape-shifter, powerful child, so we
can smell fresh cotton against our pasty cheeks,

then melt crayons into bottle caps to shoot
scullies on the hard Bronx pavement again.

On Winter Evenings Father Strings the Moon

It tags along behind us tallowing maples
draped in frosted capes. The six o'clock
whistles long and low, long and low. Over snow

we trek in silence through hollows
of our town. Does quiet keep us quick?
An eagle shadows us so low
we can hear the whoosh of wings
until he leads us to twin steeples
where he pierces sky mocking

Orion's sword. In the cemetery
behind the church, Joshua, Ezechial
and Abigail sleep, warmer than we

who stamp our feet and clap our hands.
Tiptoeing over opal quilts spread
on loamy cradles, we trace

their names and dates on stones
listing like tilted sails. Hand in hand,
we, a trinity, then trudge home listening

to crunch of brittle snow, listening to tiny heart-
beats, ripe berries bursting in blue fire.

The House That Ruth Built

In front of a hole in the right field wall
my father spreads the tarpaulin to protect
the grounds from a sudden downpour.

His once slender waist now bulges like
the Babe's, too many center-cut pork chops
and home-grown spuds. On his forearm, a tattoo,

Hands Across the Sea, two hands shaking
over the red, white and blue, the green, white
and gold, a tryst between Ireland and America.

With a North-Irish brogue, he'd tell us
they lament the loss of the old country
where they hadn't a flute to jig to,

this is the greatest country in the world
and don't you forget it.
As if forgetting how he'd gotten these afternoons

at the stadium: the truck owner, a well-connected Yank,
one hand washing the other, I guess, who bestowed
that job upon him after its wheels crushed

his five-year-old son's head, a job he kept
through the Golden Age of Baseball
'til the New York, New Haven and Hartford,

a pensioned position, beckoned. In lieu of his son's blues
he saw Lou Gehrig's weep, his brittle voice
bouncing off the bleachers and Dimaggio's velvets

squint in the two o'clock sun, his hands sheltering them
as though he were saluting. At home,
thirty blocks south, we baked scones to the tattoo of the kettle

and the drone of Mel Allen's loamy *Going, going, gone.*

Picking Up Steam

My father was a car knocker,
the handmaiden of the locomotive
as it rested, sweated in the Oak Point yard,
en route to Hartford and New Haven.
After his calloused fingers secured
her pistons, bolts, and screws,
he'd rap his iron wrench
on her corrugated door signaling
her safety to the engineer.

Royal, magisterial, her black-velvet flanks
illuminated by the fat summer moon,
she'd snort smoke, whistling her high soprano,
Tirnagog kicking up pebbles,
. looping the American miles.
And my father, an immigrant,
ebonized by her grease,
a part of it, a part of it, a part of it.

On the Day My Father's Father Died

the message scudded across the sea
and hovered like cumulus over him

as he cradled his head in his arms
on our kitchen table and bled.

I had never seen him
who had already buried a son,

as a son, in a field squashing hay mice
as his father threshed, or helping his father

carve soles to glue onto their sodded boots.
A father he never blamed

for his own frailities as his well-shod
American children would fault him.

For the first time I understood his grief
and cherished the small boy in him

as he plodded towards the railroad
his tin lunch box like a small black barn.

I Longed to Be as Lovely

as Sister Purissima in her opal linen gown
her tanned cheeks backlit by her veil

like an angel surprised, longed to script
the green alphabet above her head

in elegant loops, to gesticulate like her:
fingers to cheek when pleased,

over her mouth when not. In her alto voice
I longed to say, *How dreary to be somebody!*

How public like a frog—I never thought about unused eggs
or night screams sewn into silent corners

or being driven insane like Theresa of Lisieux
by another nun's beads clicking against oak.

Mary has chosen the better part and it will not be taken from her.
Luke 10:42

Awakened by the mourning of Harlem
River fog horns, groggy, I peeked through
the black window guard over the fence
into the concrete yard where twenty-one nuns
billowed like black sails into early mass
in the gray haze. I slipped
my wool sweater over my pajama top and toweled
the sleep from my eyes. I abandoned my hollow
-cheeked mother to the cowled baby howling in the cradle
and dashed to kneel behind their domed veils,
shoulder-to-shoulder, a medieval flank, candles radiant
like saved souls before them. Woozy
from my midnight fast, in an incensed swoon,
I longed to sneak into their hallowed heaven, wound
in white linen, unaware dark habits lurked there, too.

Great Expectations

It was always up to us, Sister said
lauding eleven-year-old
Beata Maria Goretti as a model,
slashed dead rather than surrender her purity.
As if we who wanted to be good
could guard the locks stemming floods
which would engulf us all.

On the Lexington Avenue Local
memorizing amo, amas, amat,
while hugging steel poles,
we were crushed by fine-suited gents
who sought out trim navy blue virgins,
our elbows a pointless defense as trains
undulated to rhythms of the morning rush.

And how could we be expected to keep saying no
as our blue-tied reflection careened
through shadowy tunnels into Manhattan
when even Joltin' Joe, *La Bella Figura,*
hooked up with Marilyn who never said no,
her vanilla skirt billowing like a parachute
pulling her towards heaven.

For My Best Friend 1950

In the cellar was buried the dismembered body
of the cherry-cheeked child butchered by the super of 598.
And even though I thought it a myth to keep girls like me
tethered, I still hugged
the curb as I skipped by. And hugged
it even more closely on that day in June
when your father and mine
bolted up the slate stairs to the roof bellowing,
Get the bastard, get the bastard. Pressing my flesh
against ochre stucco, I, wall-eyed and slack-jawed,
saw your trembling five-year-old body
brindled by the ruby rays of the stairwell's
stained glass, your flaxen hair buried
in your mother's corn-flowered house coat,
the X of her arms like crossed swords guarding you.

Casting Aspersions

Hard to tell what the woman did
to deserve being hooked
to a chair attached to a wooden paddle
dunked in a deep pond in a feral forest,
her brown gown a fishing trawl,
sun-shimmered, her mouth a gash.
Bearded men in sad-colored garments
and black, steeple-crowned hats swirl about, carp.

Bobbing left to right, left to right
on the wrought iron treadle
of my mother's Singer
I look at the woman in a book as big as myself.
What fault hers? Singing too
loud in chapel, a lace petticoat peeking
beneath her skirt, a wayward glance cast? Masked
we ride the Singer's iron hump like Heigh-Ho-Silver
or spin its wheel over treacherous cliffs.

My mother has nothing to call her own.

In his over-stuffed chair my father laments
my brother Butchie,- -Whisht!--
a name I rarely hear, accusing
--accusing, accusing who--my mother dunking spuds
in roiling water? Himself? I bury
my face in her lap gasping for air.
In Hitchcock's *I Confess*,
Montgomery Clift-- a priest accused
of a murder he's absolved, declines to break
his silence, must live maligned like Hester, for that crime.

My Friends Had Nothing

In the Mullaly home there was no
beef stew simmering on the stove
a smell so full it could pull you up
three flights of stairs on a spider's thread.
Nor were there eggs shimmering in bacon fat
so thick Excalibur could have risen from it.

After the 8:30 mass on Sunday
there were promises of biscuits conjured
with the rim of a glass and gingerbread
topped by cream whipped by silver wands
til its peaks made you whoop.
Billy and Henry waited, pretended the potted pothos
gagging on its own weeds was cactus.

They, Custer's advance, trilled their golden bugles
miracles to the women and children choking in the circle
of covered wagons, their ribs already ablaze
until the boys heard the crack too early
on the Sabbath from the can in their father's hand
the drag of the kitchen chair their weathered mother
stood on, the Seagram's on the shelf for herself
hid from their father the night before.

Death Reels

Men's faces floated beneath grey fedoras,
as they entered the lobby of my building
through the side door of Mulligan's
Funeral Home. Candles cast puppets
on hot summer nights, as painted lips
and tangerine cheeks popped like plums
from satin-upholstered caskets.

In daylight, we, the privileged of 615,
dared Julie from 622 to peer through a chink
in the cellar door to see Mr. Mulligan
suck fluids from the dead through straws,
sew their eyes shut with chicken sinew
and starch their hair into cotton candy.
Death had an orange glow.

In school we lauded eleven-year-old
Beata Maria Goretti slashed dead
rather than render her purity.
At home my father sang of Kevin Barry
who *in a lonely Brixton prison*
high upon a gallow's tree
gave his young life for the cause of liberty.

Dear God, didn't anyone want us to live?

Julie threw up by the firehouse door
a fireman straddling a wooden milk crate
flicked his Lucky Strike ashes into the air.

How I Loved the Way Sister Hooked Up

her floor length linen scapular
into her black leather belt and cuffed
her balloon sleeves to keep them clean.

As our last classmate skipped out
the door to summer, my buddy and I
filled a porcelain pan with bubbly water

and scrubbed each desk erasing
inky archives of another year. Ripping
paper bag covers from books

we stacked spellers and math texts
into ordained spots lonely since September.
Stripped of flawless essays festooned

with johnny jump-ups we had cut out
to hasten Spring, bulletin boards paled.
Then for the last time in fifth grade

on the third floor fire escape
we conjured huffy ghosts
with clapped erasers as June sun hazed

us for completing another year, a small
ritual built into our brittle lives. Sadness
settled over me as I whispered goodbye to

Sister alone in that sterile room not knowing
if I could ever love that much again.

Part Two

The Florist Gave Me Gifts

Like confetti, alizarin crimson, viridian, burnt
sienna, bamboo green, rose madder

petals spilled from buckets onto gray concrete.
Sweet bouquet! No matter how late I ran

from the subway, I'd dash into Mr. Tree's
grotto, where he'd pluck gladiolas, camellias,

sweet peas or mums, wire them tight,
attach a matching bow, or else

wrap roses or lilies in sleek long boxes
anyone would be happy to receive.

Young and late for class I was beguiled by such beauty,
hustled from Chelsea peddlers 20 blocks away

—not from Brazilian jungles or equatorial Africa
where bare-breasted women stronger than the Nile

balanced baskets on their heads—I longed to be
a florist or a baker or even a shoemaker

where smells and sights were so inebriating
people loved you just for letting them close.

The Life You Save

His mother, a stranger, henna hair unkempt,
lists like shook foil into our Saturday morning
whirlwind of spic and spanning. Slurring syllables,
she begs my father for cash. He warns me
never again to see her son, a lifeguard
who slips off the brass rail the first time
he sees me at St. Mary's Park Pool.

Sixteen, he salvages his flotsam family, works nights,
slices deli meat weekends for rent and cheap eats.
He pilots his math-nut brother and frets
for his pistol sister. His ballast
is his music: *Carousel, Pinafore, Butterfly* and Jerry Lee;
his treasure scuttled one night by his mother's errant match.
I, too, forsake him. Later, he drinks, fights fires,
jettisons charred cadavers, the stench of burning
vinyl still reeks from all his pores.

Saturday at F. W. Woolworth's

Steam rose from a silver crescent hood
sterilizing white plates and swallowing cutlery.
The silver goose-necked fountain honked
and caged canaries sang. Hair-netted,
I crated and emptied, crated and emptied
then nickle-and-dimed BLT's:
one strip broken into four bits,
a tomato slither, a pinch of mayo,
lettuce laid on rye toast dipped in
grease served with coffee, cherry coke,
or an egg cream to my boss, Mr. D'Amboise,
whom we dubbed *Fang,* leering from the edge
of the counter, and to neighborhood
shoppers who gossiped and left small tips.

I loved the small talk, the girls' scarfed hair
set in bobby-pin grids of perfect X's,
the teenage boys swiping
dog chains, the ache in my lower back,
the mustard-clogged funnels, loved
even my father who tipped
his tweed cap after eats, ' *Twas grand*, he'd say
then stiffed me as he spun from his red leather stool.

Sunday at the German Bakery

Oh beatific toffee-eyed boy
who when you clerked at the bakery

I, weak from my midnight fast,
bought white mountain rolls after mass

for my family's morning feast
of bacon and eggs. At three I returned,

sweet as a linzer tart, smokey as a mocha layer
purchased for dessert after fricasseed

chicken fit for Tristan or a toffee-eyed boy
who clerked at a bakery, slipping his fingers in and out

tying the knot on the white box. Before you closed,
I, brittle as an egg shell, came

back for crusty seeded rye un-sliced,
and a quart of pasteurized milk

hoping it would conjure scenes of lovers
sifting thru fields of wheat.

Ran out, I'd say, *Knead you, I, uh, mean, them*
for school lunches and breakfast, only store open,

a half-baked lie, the deli next to the firehouse
lit up, a few doors down, open til ten.

Oh beatific toffee-eyed boy, bakery clerk
once we stood shoulder to elbow

on the subway like olives stuffed in a loaf,
aromas of chocolate and almond-crunch wafting,

surely a sign from He Who Cannot Be Named
destined to be hot-crossed lovers nibbling

apple cobbler, yolked together
hobbling along until the glaze wears off.

Holy Day

Prim in my proper dress, I sat
seventh period, red-lining Latin roots: puer-puerile,

amo-amiable, rex-regalia. The anemic November sun
blanched the library's tomes as Lincolnesque

Mr. Stollmeyer listed in, pale as parchment
The president has been shot, he said.

We placed our fingers over our mouths
as if testing for breath How will we tell

our students? It was the feast of St. Cecelia,
the patroness of music, a pewter harp in hand.

Forced to marry, she remained a virgin and converted
Valerian. Unwilling to worship Roman idols

she was thrown into a vat of boiling oil for burying
the bodies of believers rather than let the vultures peck

out their souls and dice their livers like dreck.
Unlike Jack, she escaped unscathed, sweet notes

floating from her throat like swallows. I wonder
if the witty, handsome Jack could sing, recite

his Latin declensions, say his evening prayers. Once,
playing chicken, he cycled headlong into his brother

Joe, flew into the air, floated-until the whoosh, the blow
to the head, sharp and surprising and painful.

Relax, he told himself, twenty-eight stitches woven into his shock
of wheat-colored hair. Too late for stitches now.

His father told him he had the goods. My mother
always said, *No good comes to those who warm their hearth*

by peddlin' poteen. The siren of the fire engine
roaring by muffled the message on the loudspeaker.

For Once I Am Able to Save Her

I thought my mother blessed to be born
and raised in a country without dentists
until the year they yanked out all her teeth.
Pearl headstones fell each week.

Now her false teeth swim in a blue Aegean
atop the porcelain sink; I remember
her mouth stuffed with bloodied cotton,
and wonder how she survived the rumbling
subway home. For her torture, I blamed dwarfish
Mrs. Hegel, the clinic's Mengele,
who cowed both dentists and patients,
shooting orders at her gap-toothed son,
her raven-haired go-fer,
his shriveled arm dangling like a light pull.

Twice a year I huddled inside those white-
washed walls, eating ether, falling backwards,
blinded by rays of a florescent sun.

Now in my dream the light shines in Kilcoo
where Mama falls backwards into the waters
of the mountain stream spilling by her cottage.
I dive, my arms cradled, breaking her fall
the skin of her back as opaline as a baby moon.

A Hot Time

You hardly want to remember when
we popped corn in Crisco in that stove-top pot,
the scorched kernels stuck to its bottom
which we would try to hide
though we couldn't hide the acrid odor
perfuming our apartment. At midnight
Pop returned from the railroad
sniffing the wind, dragged us out of bed
because we hadn't even washed
the dishes and had we tried to burn the house down
in the bargain, too? I'd snarl I had been asleep
even though I 'd been translating Cicero
under the sheets with a flashlight,
homework which I had not started until
after late-night Steve Allen recited a letter
to the editor from Vox Populi in The Daily News
like it was *I must rise and go now to the Isle of Innisfree.*

Then Michael would rat and say he hadn't done his spelling
because I had refused to help him which I did
because our sessions commanded by
Sister Caritas had ended in a brouhaha. Years later
we'd blame Pop for all our hang ups as we micro waved
crisp, tasteless corn in a disposable bag. After he died
he'd pop out of the dish water like a genii asking me
if I had had my heels repaired, *You can tell a man's*
character by the shape of his shoes and tell corny jokes
about my *clutie* feet. Downstairs Mrs. Garrido sealed our fate
by popping a complaint into our mailbox

about how Fats Domino had been belting out
he'd found his thrill on Blueberry Hill
through the open windows all night.

Tonight I Let My Brother In

He has been tapping on my window for years.
Tonight I let him in the door,

his blue eyes still sure, his pony legs still strong,
his hardscrabble voice startling.

He removes his Yankee baseball cap,
his salt and pepper hair thick as Pop's.

Still, I think how he tore his father's life asunder
by his early death. He flops and flings his arm

on the back of my couch as if he owned it.
Why are you still here?

Because I'm your big brother, I've lingered light years.

He tosses his cap on my head. From it,
the smell of honeysuckle pours down on me.

How you would have loved me, Sister, if we'd had more time.

Part Three

Fat in the Can

On the shady back porch of his summer home,
Uncle Dan, even and easy like my mother,
constructs a lamp from wooden matchsticks.
Calls me Crisco. I am eleven,
in t-shirt and shorts, and click my Wrigley's.
I cringe and shrink from him. Nine years later,
as I take the novice's white veil, he stands next to me,
my starved body swallowed by the folds
of a lily-colored linen gown and scapular,
my thick hair shorn, my face as pallid as a scone.

At five the Sisters chose me to crown the Virgin
Queen of the May. She was elegant,
imperially slim, unlike my full-breasted mother,
whisking the stir-about, mewling babies on each hip.
Her brother Dan, still single, reading *The Daily News*,
slurps cereal and sips from a china cup
the tea she brewed for him. She was a slave.
Each day in school the Virgin loomed above us
her exquisite hands outstretched, index finger
beckoning me. One by one we dropped
our daisies pressing each petal to our lips.

Rose Hawthorne* Creates

Unlike my father, Nathaniel's, words
mine scuttled like tangled limbs

on the page until a cancerous seamstress,
leaven for rats in an East Eleventh gutter,

stirred my muse. Before she was quarantined
on Blackwell's Island, I cleansed pus

from her stippled scabs, dripped honey
on her blistered lips, lay her rotting shell

on soft white sheets. Her breath's last vibration,
a vine of ivy I wove into grace which spun

my work of solace into breathless prose.

*Founder of the Dominican Sisters of the Sick Poor

Teresa of Avila, Mystic, Reformer, Exhorts Her Sisters

I, a bare-foot, foot-loose pilgrim,
wandered in the heavy Castilian air,
took bread when sick from the pierced hands of Christ.

And thus, Sisters, I know you can do this,
you can surrender your leather zapatos,
the brooches pearling your beads, your perros
fatted on roasted beef yelping in your laps.

For you, I, have slept in lice-infested inns,
endured lawsuits and venomous gossip,
fenned off the Doña with the patch o'er her eye.

Soon I will shed this flimsy carcass
and its sweet odor searing your nostrils
will move the worldly fools who need saints
to do strange things.
                              La vida es sueño.

Tell them, Sisters, mi corazón, now encased
in jeweled rock-crystal, an angel
once pierced with a gold-tipped arrow.

They will enshrine my emerald-ringed finger
on the cathedral altar in Avila. Later Franco
will sleep with my left hand by his side.

Stunned by Charismatics at Evening Mass

Led by an out-of-habit nun,
twenty students
in the rough-hewn Fordham chapel
encircle a young man in tight jeans
who has begged for healing.

Jesus bless him, they cry, *Jesus heal him*
restore him, oh blessed Jesus.
Yes Jesus yes. Allelulia. My knees tremble
needy with laughter.

Who are these people?

Come, help us pray, she says.
How surprising to find
myself in a huddle of huggers
with my hand on his shoulder.
Jesus!
As I exit the chapel, I mutter
in the autumn gloaming
crunch leaves underfoot
as street lamps flick on
like struck matches
and shed light on tears
rilling down my cheeks.

A Wife to Her Dying Husband

Get on with it now
y' auld blatherskite.
Aren't we that sick of lookin'
at each other for forty years.
Twenty thousand cups of tea together.
Enough boiled spuds chomped
to feed a legion of Black and Tans.
A bit of quiet t' wouldn't be a bother.
' Tis your moanin' in Belial's night
I cannot thole.
Hurry now, tear thru the blue lights
a lamb needs to be suckled—

My Old Man Couldn't Even Die Quiet

On Fridays, taking two steps to his one,
I'd walk with him to the Red House
under the Triborough Bridge to pick up his check.

He'd never pass anyone he knew without a word
and he knew them all: Garrity, Condemi,
Monsignor, the baker, the shoemaker.

His words buzzed over my head like locusts.
I'd shift from one foot to the other.
His syllables filled craters of loss:
the Depression, the Mountains of Mourne,
his father Mick, three infants, his five year old son.

One day he closed the garden gate behind him,
took the El to the old neighborhood,
never got time to talk about it.

He didn't come home. We were the ones
who talked and talked and talked
who called and called and called.

Offering

Fluff white towels
and place a wash cloth by the sink.
Snap the white sheet
and smooth its corners into small gifts.
Cover it with a white spread
and fold over its hem.
Plump white pillows
and place them beneath his head.
In the chipped cup set pyracantha
in praise of him.

Beware lest he pricks his finger
which will bleed
like the huge red ball
you will pull down
from the sky until it sinks out of sight
until it is a line behind
a blue-hulled boat
luffing beneath a cloud.

Caught Unaware

When he rested his first born
against his solid chest

bare flesh against bare flesh
he knew she was the sweet

that would feed all his days.
He doused his last smoke,

dumped his last Dewar's
ferried her in a shopping bag

to present her to his sister.
Then father and daughter

feasted at Shepherd's Lake,
heard carillons chime

as they inhaled the mauve heave
of May's earth, watched a vermilion sun

settle like butter between hollows
of screed hills where skeet shots

cleaved silence and red-winged blackbirds
squabbled like kin below.

Driving to School on This Most Amazing Day

Maybe the blinding sun or the shadows
cast by the lacy girders of the bridge
dazzled me as I glided east on the GWB.
Maybe someone clipped my right rear fender
spinning my Reliant into the left lane,
a sixteen-wheeler hurtling towards me.
Huit clos.
My head thumps, thumps, thumps
to the soothing radio rhythms
of the Reverend Bob Cook.
                        I knew I was about to die,
was grateful I had lived to see my children grown,
saw my students sullen ' cause I didn't show,
annoyed I had just paid the toll.
Suddenly my car halted, my front wheels
                resting on the edge of the bridge,
the sixteen-wheeler, five feet away, towering over me
neighing like Boanerges. Two construction workers
in plaid wool shirts tapped on my window,
Are you ok, lady? Are you ok?
                        Am I ok? Am I ok?
                        Are any of us ever ok?
The Reverend Bob Cook signing off,
Walk with the King today and be a blessing.

The Man Who Loved His Mother-in-Law

In the late afternoon after work he dropped
in on her as the city sun slipped down

like a halo behind where she drifted off
in a wing chair wrapped in an afghan

she knitted, a newspaper spread on her lap.
He named his first child for her. In her nineties

he interviewed her for hours on video tape
where she spoke of the death of her five

year-old-son and how though pregnant nine times,
she never liked sex much. Three babies died.

We don't speak of such things, she said.
But she did, to him, for us.

The August Place

Mister Conklin's bay-hugged, dusty cottage
with the mildewed corner cot

in the small white room but not
too small for us who lay

hip to hip in it. Warm smooth skin
and misty breath. Salt-encrusted eaves.

The breezed, gauzy curtains billowing
above our heads. The sweet silence

of your shirtless self. Your crooked-up
arm beneath your head and I, yoked,

as we whispered in the hollow space of
Mister Conklin's bay-hugged, musty cottage.

Summer's demise would soon catch us
off guard and always we'd be heartsick for it.

A brown hair spare on a pillow
a red-winged blackbird window-ledged.

My Second Pair of Eyes

Pull down the moon, I say, *and smother it*
in down. Light stirs sleep. *Even dark*

needs light, my love says, when we quibble
over light and color. I fancy rooms

plumed in hemlock, burgundy and cobalt blue.
He brushes them white: ecru, eggshell, opal,

pearl. I had forgotten Teresias, blind seer

ignored by Creon to his woe. I had forgotten

my love's double vision, letters pirouetting
on the page, his long lashes shading eyes of umber.

What I Did Not Say

From the steps of her house,
late afternoon light candling her hair,

my sister and I overlook Cupsaw Lake
where her six children swam

and flourished like local fauna.
She tells me to tell her husband

the house looks great. He wants to sell,
too much work, wants to tee off in Florida.

Before I leave, she says she speaks everyday
to John, a friend, who died last year.

She laughs, *I'll be joining him soon.*
Rushing, I check my bag for my keys,

my wallet, my makeup case,
give her a hug and am stung

by her bones protruding like nettles.
Good days, bad days, she says.

I look at her. I did not want to hear
what I did not say.

Interruptions

Why is it in the middle of sex
this poem begins to mushroom in my head?

How, as a child, I chose Elizabeth of Hungary as my patron saint,
when I could have chosen Elizabeth, Mary's cousin,

surely more of a direct line to You-Know-Who. And, she,
prestigious enough to be honored in a mystery of the rosary.

Was it because the Hungarian was a queen?
And when her King forbade her visits to the poor,

(Now I realize perhaps like Browning's Last Duchess, the King
thought
she liked whatever she looked on, and her looks went everywhere.)

she went anyway hiding the piping hot loaves of bread
under her red velvet cloak, and meeting the King

on his steed, he demanded she open it.
She obeyed and a forest of roses fell at his feet:

double burgundies, dusky wine, mottled violet,
mauve, burnt sienna and moss maroon.

When my sister—my second mother—died
I knew it was the feast of my patron saint.

Anxious to see my sister on the mend, as the oncologist
had predicted, I had already packed my bags.

And when I heard the phone ring too early
on that chilly feast, I crumpled on the top of the stairs.

In her eulogy I spoke of the scarlet fever
she survived when young, all of us quarantined.

And of the oil she painted in high school, a cloudburst
of tiny purple violins floating on a field of white.

Virtue Rewarded

Using her teeth to open the U of bobby pins,
my sister Ann secured her hair into pinwheel rows
each marked by a perfect X.

I'd cut out *Brenda Starr,* wonder
if I could ever weave such virtue.
And when bull-like Danny Garrido pulled

my twisted braids, she deflated him with a look.
Years later when I snatched her angora sweater
for a Friday night dance she caught me

seeing it askew on her silk-quilted hanger.
Though engaged twice, she never married.
Each night she herded the wobbly letters

of her tiny students like The Good Shepherd
shouldering a lamb. She cared for
mother til the end slamming her bedroom door

in my face that night in the hospital
when I'd abandoned mother
to a ghoulish nurse on the graveyard shift.

I would have come had you called, Ann said,
as if her vigil would have drained the lake
rising in her lungs. My mother died without me,

her mouth a bit crooked, her needle-pricked
hand resting against my sister's damp cheek.

What Is Hardest

is being the last to go
outliving husband, siblings, daughter
and Mary Monk with whom she consumed

scampi and pasta e fagioli at Meoli's after mass.
At 95 she still fricassees chicken, grows plump
crimson tomatoes and bright green snap peas,

ties the last knot in a rug
she hooks and knocks off Maeve Binchy
in an afternoon. She pines for her peers,

her memory menage, who torched along
with Sophie Tucker, the last
of the red hot mamas, *Some one of these days,*

you're gonna miss me, honey. During the Depression,
they had to take turns sleeping in creaky beds
at Aunt Kate's. They relished Mickeys exploded

over trash-can fires in the gold-paved gutters
of the then not so Big Apple.
On the calendar, she marks Mary's anniversary,

the feast of the Conversion of Paul, a lightning-bolted
profligate, blinded, then thrown by his horse,
whom Jesus asked, *Saul, Saul, why dost thou persecute me?*

She sighs, nods, even though she can no longer walk
to the market alone, her purse purloined once
her eyes misjudging the height of curbs.

Lessons

In her cabbage-flowered housecoat she clutches
the silver canister beneath her heart,

tosses a fist full of leaves into the Delft pot,
then douses them with sizzling water.

"You have to let it seep," she says.
Her hands hold the Blue Willow

cup painted with two Chinese lovers
plotting on a wooden bridge; she mostly listens.

Then she tips my empty cup:
in the leaves she sees a black-haired man

she warns me not to marry and the blood-red boat
we will sail on in and out of seas

and over weeks and years. It is wise
to wait and to be silent.

Tranquility has granted her ninety-six years
and when, near the end, her lungs flushed with fluid,

a nurse serves her weak yellow tea not fit for pigs,
in the leaves a howling wolf,

she turns her cup upside down
and sets its rim in the round lip of the saucer.

.

Part Four

Early Sorrow

After the three sisters had waited nine months
for the baby who was born dead,
they fretted about her being buried alone.
So they placed next to her
their almost-favorite stuffed animals,
the toucan by her plump cheeks
and the kookaburra by her elbow.
In her hands, they put the board book
Good Night Gorilla, in which the gorilla-hero steals
the keys from the zookeeper's belt,
and frees the elephant, lion and giraffe.
The sisters knew she would laugh
when the animals followed the keeper to his house,
and the gorilla slept in his bed.
Plus she would learn about locks and keys.
And when Grandma died seven days later,
they knew she would read the book to the baby
and blow on her belly and sing
Toora, Loora, Loora.
                    These are the things
the three sisters did and told us,
the grown ups who did nothing, but sit
like stones in our chairs, staring.

The Healing

Like the Orkney Islanders, my daughter dreams
seals are human. In a rush-bottomed boat

her infant—born dead—floats over weeks through years
in and out of seas lolling on waves, uillean pipes pealing.

A brown-eyed seal suckles her with breast milk
so rich it raises inches of fat on her;

black moons peer from a cave until the tide
recedes. On every midsummer's eve

every ninth night, every seventh stream
the infant clears the water and slips her skin

down to the sand like an old coat. She skips
and twirls on lonely stretches of pearl-lit shore.

The Child Inside the Mirror

A sprite in an iris pinafore skirts past me.
Was it my second-born child years ago
slipping by me at the kitchen sink
as I dipped my rosy hands in soapy water?
Steam rose through the early light
streaming through the frosted window.

I sensed she was myself brushing
by my mother reading the tea leaves
in the bottom of her rose-spotted cup.

Or was it my daughter's first born
her umbilical cord rosaried about her neck?
She shivers in the ice cold frame, whispering,
I am. Here I am. Here. I am here.

Dos Diablos

Like two old lushes spilling
out of the swinging doors of a saloon

Mikey, fourteen months, and David,
two and a half, besotted by their own guffaws,

bump heads and pot-bellies. On the porch
Mikey pings cat pellets and David

huzzahs him on. Under the coffee table
each one stretches the cat, one by his tail, the other by his ears.

Their ears glued to the seats of red plastic chairs,
they skid around the track of the living room, dining room and

kitchen screeching and scratching memories into the varnished oak.
They tug *Where the Wild Things Are* until Sendak squeals.

We call them *Dos Diablos, Hermanos de Sangre*
but soon the younger will outstrip the older.

The first day Mikey realizes David speaks
five words to his fifty, realizes David still flops

down the stairs on his butt Mikey will become
big brother, el jefe, as he reads *Wild Things*

to David who still shimmies, hands over head, to *Wooly Bully*.

My Three Year Old Grandson Has Down

The red and yellow Tonka truck
that he had laid his chest on

and pushed with short legs two blocks
is parked parallel to my car.

David, how did you get here alone? I say.
My five year old brother's crushed skull

flashes by. *I must call your mother.*
He dashes into the computer room,

bangs on the keys, laughs at the rainbow screen.
I laugh, too, recalling the day I heard him

using the mouse as a phone.
He winds the red-knobbed handle

moving the tin merry-go-round, and
claps when the farmer and wife

circle in and out of the door.
He tosses Tinker Toys from their small turret

to hear the screak of wood on oak.
Bodacious boy who knows no danger,

who slipped into this world
on a thread as fine as a banshee's cry,

67

how will we protect you from the drifter
whistling under the street light,

the bully who spits in your milk,
the sweet flotsam of yourself.

Grace

The mother leans into her young son,
six feet tall, dressed in black tee and jeans,
strapped into a wheelchair,
spoons tapioca into his mouth,
her fingers extended
as if she is creating a morning sky.

Could I have her patience?

Short smooth strokes master quick drying paint:
alizarin crimson, viridian, Prussian blue,
The sun soars above the stark white sails of a red boat.

The Fall

After a bachelor's bash
for his sister's intended
at the Taj Mahal, Jake,
the best man, dumps his buddies,
misplaces his room, snoozes
on the hood of his car
in the rooftop garage.

At four a.m.
he slides off like hot butter
descends to hollow earth below.

Caught on security tape, he beams
as if he were jack knifing,
slicing air. At the last
he throws back his head,
his mouth a split persimmon,
reaches out to catch
his sister's scopic, ringless hand.

Sleep Over Parties

As the 200th sheep hurls herself
off the cliff, I, a menopausal insomniac,
feel like a butcher
who weeps over bloody piles
yet cannot help but conjure towers
of succulent loin and center cuts.
Clearly, counting is not working.
So I gather wool which
now I pull over my eyes.
But still the sheep
I have known plea before me:
Baa, baa, black sheep carries three bags full.
Mary's little lamb follows her
to school. The Sheep in a Jeep drive like goats.
Issac's sub lays down his life
for a friend. Where is the Good
Shepherd now that His lost sheep needs him
to throw Sleep over His shoulder and bring him
to my verdant pasture. In wolf's clothing
Sleep perches cross-pawed on the edge
of my bed puffing smoke halos
above his head. *Old habits die hard,*
he says; his mutton lips mock my count.

In My Dream

a gangly stranger galumphs
down my stairs, a cross
between Bela Lugosi and Elwood P. Dowd
in *Harvey*. Though I sense doom I feign
friendliness, *Did my husband rent
the upstairs to you?* I think
of Elwood's advice, *I used to be smart
but nice is better.* I try to be both.
My granddaughter doesn't smell the danger.
I small talk.
Should I tell her to bolt for the door?

But then I will be left alone with this
villain whom I know will swat me
like a mosquito. I wish that Harvey,
a six-foot pookah, would appear.

Dry-mouthed, I awake, a whiff of decay
and spirits waft over me.
I check locks on windows and doors,
contemplate buying a gun.
I know it's my fear of my granddaughter's
flowering and of the bees that buzz about her.
I fear the wolf in rented fleece, the gandy dancers,
the *amathons* my father could not thole,
the honey-tongued galoots in zoot suits.

The Lady of Annie B Street is Gone

Ninety-five-year-old Nellie Mulligan,
an amber-eyed munchkin,
outspoke her preacher husband
by fifteen hundred Sundays. Still dead-
heading her portulaca and roasting
green peppers from her garden
until her hard-of-hearing son
whisked her from under the canopy
of copper beech, each planted at the birth
of a child. He sold her helter-skelter house
the walls still battle-ship green,
their holes stuffed with Wrigley's.
Then he died six months later
leaving Nellie rudderless. Shipped
to a nursing home where she pined
for sea gulls shrieking,
                  her starched sails fluttered
                  flimsily as silk.

How to Deconstruct a Home

Like his ramshackle homilies
preacher Mulligan fabricated

his graceless cottage by the sea
adding on one room at a time.

Laying asbestos tiles he belittled
Nellie, his wife, who sought refuge

on her knees among foxglove, broad beans
and yellow squash. Built too close to the ground

now floors sag like worn out phrases
tree roots choke pipes like calumnies.

The ochre bulldozer bludgeons
the red shingled roof, eats the war-surplus-

painted walls for breakfast
the windows for lunch

the pipes for supper
then chews and scatters the remains.

By nightfall Nellie's ghost keens
not for her preacher but for her

salt-encrusted cottage, her gone-to-seed
garden. Her billowing skirt

luffs over the churned plot
like a shrouded sail.

The White-Washed Cottage

I open the door
enter the old house
the bold closeness
of the silence clots the air.

His army fatigue hangs
on a hook, elbows creased from use,
his Donegal cap laps over it.

At any moment you expect him
to grab the tweed and slap it
on his silvered head
tug the fatigue about his shoulders
his gravelly treble echoing,

I'm off.

The Spelling Test

Teach your brother to spell
Sister Caritas said.
So each night Michael and I
fifteen months apart, sparred
at the enamel table over
i before *e* and double *b*'*s*.

How I relished folding up
my sleeves like Sister,
tossing my braids
as if they were a veil
and stabbing his *decieve*,
occassion and *bubles*
with my red pen.

He'd rip the papers to shreds
and convert them to confetti.
Each session ended in poisoned barbs,
You dumb ox, I'd hiss.
Ass kisser, he'd sneer.

Today through a trach,
my brother spits out muddled syllables
his left side paralyzed, his lips trembling.
When I massage his neck and shoulders
I test him still,
Where are my fingers, I ask.
Here,
  here
    or there?

The House on Overing Street

No one is there
who was there before.
We knock on the door.
Strangers answer; horses
rear in the courtyard
clop on cobblestones
bare their teeth.
All are wary of us
huddling in the dark hall.
We speak in tongues
and no one touches
the hand of the other.

What does the soul do for solace then?
Memory dissipates
like a withered wreath.
What you thought was, isn't.
        You no longer are
what you thought you were.
            How fast it all goes—
            How fast the water rises.
You hear the altered voice
of another coming from your throat—

Words Sprout Wings

At first the white lie I told alighted
like a firefly: an excuse about caring

for my sick friend. Then her name appeared
on sides of trucks, on oatmeal boxes, on spines of books.

Her face cropped up on a preying mantis
stuck to a screen. I found her among red blossoms

in a terra cotta pot, among lipstick and eye liner
in my pink case by the sink. I found her

in the hollow where my wisdom tooth used to be.
I heard her in the chicken wings crackling in the pan

in the crunch of boots on hard snow, in the corn
popping in the microwave like a Quaker bonnet.

Thoughts of her made my skin itch,
my eyelid twitch. When I saw her in dust

floating down from an overhead fan
as it cast its shadows on my narrow

world, I had no choice but to call her
although I did not want to hear what

I knew she was going to say.

A Secret of Long Life

In exchange for books of thirsty grids stamped S&H,
a glossy toaster popped up in Mama's kitchen,
a marvel unlike the one whose silver wings flapped
flat singeing fingers and scorching toast.

To Aunt Susannah's brood in Kilcoo,
Mama sent our outgrown clothes.
In exchange for bags and bags of rags she packed,
a carpet weaver conjured a field of acanthus leaves.
Toasty feet on bloodless Bronx mornings. Anemic
tea leaves nourished pothos and gardenia.
She spun scraped bits of beef into gravy so bronze
it made us weep. She did not take more than she gave
and thus was given long life

and a fur-collared Persian lamb coat
my sister and I bought her with our first pay checks.
Although we thought we had outgrown such thrift,
today my sister stocks up on bargains.
Neither she nor her hair will last long enough
for all those bottles of sale shampoo.
And I have begun to record purchase dates
on creams and lipsticks to tally how long they last.

About the Author

A Secret of Long Life has been nominated for the Robert McGovern Prize. Liz Dolan's first poetry collection, *They Abide,* was published by March Street. A six-time Pushcart nominee and winner of Best of the Web and finalist for Best of the Net, Liz has received an established professional in poetry fellowship from the Delaware Division of the Arts and has been chosen for residencies at The Atlantic Center for the Arts and Martha's Vineyard. She has also won fiction prizes from The Nassau Review, The Master's Review and The Cobalt Review's Baseball Poetry Prize. Liz serves on the poetry board of *Philadelphia Stories.* She is most grateful for her ten grandchildren, all of whom live one block away; they pepper her life.

About the Charity

Since 2006, the mission of the Rehoboth Beach Boardwalk Buddy Walk has been to create a community where people with Down syndrome, or any other cognitive disorder, can live, learn, work and play.

boardwalkbuddywalk.com
dennis@ boardwalkbuddywalk.com

Made in the USA
Middletown, DE
07 February 2015